T.E Henry

A Heart
Protected by God

A Coffee Table Book

Original photography by T.E Henry

Print information available on the last page

Rev. date: 06/11/2018

To order additional copies of this book, contact:
Xlibris
1-888-795-4274
www.Xlibris.com
Orders@Xlibris.com

Table of Content

Dedications

I dedicate this book to the young lady who helped me see God's love in the world once more. She saw God in me at a moment in my life that I didn't see God in myself. She took time to thank God for my presence in her life, and so today I thank God for her. Unknown to her, her sweet token of Christmas love would awaken my dreams. I had forgotten one very essential thing, that I now know and have confirmed, which is, my heart is protected by God.

*Proceeds from the sale of this book will be secured for De'Mya's college education.

I also dedicate this book to my daughter Gianna. The Purest love I have ever known, other than the love of God, is the love of my daughter. I pray life never brings her any hurt or pain, however, if it does God will be there for her and will help her in the same forgiving manner he has helped me. Thus far in my life I have never met a person so gentle, caring and loving as my daughter. Those who know and love her would agree. Thus, I dedicate this book to her because she is an earthly representation of goodness and love.

A Note to my readers

I have written this book at a moment in my life when I feel I am closet to God. I am not perfect, and I declare I am still a sinner. However I am on my journey. The lord has seen it fit to begin a good work in me, and for that I am thankful. I pray you found a poem or two in this book that has moved you, inspired you, or given you clarity in some form.

I prayed for God's guidance and asked him to allow his messages to flow through my hands as I typed. Reading his words repeatedly, I called his angels to anchor at my side. The one thought that flowed through me as I completed each poem, is the need to end immoral and unethical thoughts and actions not only in myself but I all men. Inside I am at peace, for I have bared witness of God's greatness, this book is my testimony. I declare God is good and we are blessed to bless others.

Fill Me

Fill me with your words lord,

I need to hear from you.

Fill me with your words lord,

Give me grace to carry through.

When the nights are short,

Days are long and I feel,

I am not strong,

My heart is yours to safeguard,

Fill me!

Fill me!

FILL ME!

My Light

You are my light in the night,

In the storm,

Guiding my way.

You are the light,

At the top of the Mountain,

Shinning my way.

Oh lord if it's your will,

Oh lord help me stay still.

Guide my mouth,

Guide my hands,

Guide my feet,

In your way.

Stormy Weather

Stormy weather is around the corner,

Before you know, sooner than you think,

Closer than you expect.

Depend on him in the midst of the storm,

He has been with you

Since the day you were born.

Don't try to make it on your own,

The storm is here

To make you feel alone.

Uncomfortable times

Will force you to shine,

The sun always shines behind the clouds.

Pull the Curtains Back

Let's pull the Curtains back!

Let's stop pretending!

Let's give the LORD a chance to work

And do some mending!

Let's pull the curtains back,

End the fears and mistrust.

Reveal your true self,

Believe in God's Love.

Let's pull the curtains back,

Give life a chance to reveal

Love is worth getting up and dancing,

When you allow God to lead.

Let's pull the curtains back,

And watch them blow,

Swaying like the wind

Where ever it may go.

Let's pull the curtains back,

It's time to trust and see

If love is worth the fight

For you and for me.

Forgiveness

Bend your fences today,

Tomorrow is not guaranteed.

Bend your fences today,

Love is all you need.

Beautiful spring yellow,

Blaze like flames on the ground,

Yet the fences block them out,

Their beauty cut off from the world.

Bend your fences NOW.

Take Heed!

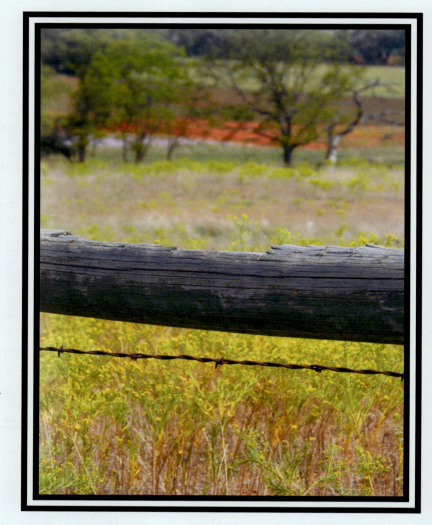

The Devil is a Liar

Ugly, nasty, unworthy,

Don't listen to him.

Remember you look like God,

And that makes the devil mad.

He wishes he were you,

He is jealous of God's love for you.

Snakes crawling from the earth,

Fire breathing dragons,

That's the path of the devil.

The devil is a liar.

He wishes he looked like us,

We are made in God's image,

We are glorious, as you can see.

Covered Under His Blood

If only one's life could be spent in this chair,

Under the umbrella shaded from the sun.

No ultra violet damage to my skin,

Covered and protected No scrapes nor blemishes.

Like an umbrella God's blood protects you.

No weapons formed against you shall stand

Nor will they decrease your latter end.

Sit here under this umbrella,

Enjoy the protection of his blood.

Watch him fight a good battle in your life.

His blood overflows, protection without end.

There is no charge for this protection,

The bill has already been paid

When Jesus died upon the cross.

Wondering Things

God might be looking down at
me through those clouds.

Even now I see his eyes staring down at me,

His brow set in a frown.

All the way up there no one but God

Would hear me scream.

If I should break under the pressure,

He would be there for me.

Those rocks,

Those hard times

Even if a whale should sallow me whole.

As the ocean looks through the Sky,

And the sky looks through the ocean,

God can see straight through me.

Get myself together, start acting right.

I had better straighten up then,

Maybe then he will turn his frown upside down.

I think I see two angels God
has sent to protect me.

They will be here soon and will
wrap me safely in their wings.

My Daughter

My daughter sleeps, and I watch her,

Wishing I had a net to catch her.

I worry for her sadness, and hope for her gladness.

Long I wait to watch her grow,

Praying to God to keep her soul.

She is a handful, she makes my heart full.

There is nothing more to say,

My daughter brings me love every day.

Hear my prayer oh lord, keep her safe.

When Called By God

Nothing could have prepared me
for the sound of his voice.

Nothing prepared me, I never had a choice.

My heart has grown so deep I long for it now,

Every echo, every whisper, every murmur

Ricochets of his lips and to my heart.

I waited all my life for his voice,

So that whence it grabbed me, I had no choice.

When he grabbed me the angles I did hear.

It's too late now, I would not turn away.

Yet now that he has given this command

My heart and soul he has in his hands.

I waited my entire life for this,

Thus now without complaint I do his will.

He calls me to love, he calls me to nurture,

He demands I bare witness and testify

This I do without hesitation, for I am called.

Talk To Him

Don't give him the
silent treatment,

Talk to him more,

Talk to him daily,

Talk until your throat is soar.

Dear God I said,

As I begun to pour out my heart,

Forgive me lord for
I have sinned.

You see my heart,

You know my faults,

And yet you love me still.

You have been a constant friend,

Even in my silence.

Lord I am lost,

I am weak and but only for you,

I would be broken.

Knowing I can turn to thee,

Knowing your love is assured,

Keeps me from breaking.

Listen to my voice Lord,

Hear me cry!

I am sorry for all these
months of silence.

I turned by back to thee,

As I willfully charged
towards the world,

Yet you never
abandoned my side.

Though now I know,

Though now I see,

And though now I acknowledge,

Hear me now,

I need you!

The Majestic Power of God

There it is,

There it stands,

The power to heal this land.

We should stare,

We should pause,

We should all stand in awe.

See it now, take it in,

Feel his power, carried on a wind.

See the sun in its grandeur,

See it wave bye, as it begins to leave the sky.

Waving happily between leaves and branches.

Night

The sun is gone from my sight,

Darkness falls, it is night.

People walk without a sight

The moon, their only flashlight.

Owling, no, but soundlessly still,

Curiously gawking at these strange things.

And should one unexpectedly look up,

The sight of four red eyes would leave them stuck.

Feet stomp quickly on their way,

The dark of the night hastening each step.

The moon's silver begins to fade,

The sun will be here soon.

Use Each Day

Beware of long cold days, that
earnest your will to be still.

Waking up with aching bones,
he wants you in bed,

Slowly stealing your soul.

For this is the day that the lord did make,

Whether snow or cold be glad in it.

Eyes wide open, seeing the delights of a new day,

Sun or snow don't let it fester away.

Pull those boat straps up, scarf
wrapped around your neck,

Inhale the cold crisp air that God has blown.

You have lived to see a new day,
for this you are blessed,

Get up, go out, and be a blessing

Until all the families of this earth are blessed.

From God
Came Many

Colors mixing is a wonderful thing.

A world without colors would be so boring.

Our differences makes us interesting.

Colors are also good for creating.

Be mindful of who is looking,

At those you are not tolerating,

At the end only one will be judging

Us all for all our sinning.

Beware of those who are hating,

The ones who do not see
colors are amazing,

Colors make the world stimulating,

Made by God for our pleasing.

Light and Darkness

God divided the light from the darkness,

He saw beauty in the light.

In one glance he saw himself,

His reflection was light

For he is the light of the world.

He is intentional,

He is all knowing,

He divided the darkness

For you to take heed,

And follow his lead.

Let there be light!

His voice echoed across the surface of the land,

Darkness was cast out,

And light began its fight,

It was all God's plan

See you now still lost,

See you now full with it,

See you now still greedy,

See you now still prideful,

Darkness still within.

Victor Not Victim

God's blood is your victory,

You cry for him to
cover you in it.

Yet, you cry for a childhood

You never lived.

Covered with his blood,

You are no longer a victim,

Less he washes it away

And you feel the sting.

If you are indeed covered
under his blood,

You are a Victor NOT a victim.

Control your thoughts,

Cast off the victim label.

Cain thought he was a victim

Look at what he did to Abel.

The devil wants to have you,

If you let him succeed,

You will lose the blood
Victory of God

And be trapped in
the devil's wings.

Rebuke the devil
from your side,

Break the victim chain

Let your tongue proclaim

You are no-longer enslaved.

I am strong!

Let your tongue bless the world

Let it be known to all,

You are covered in
victorious blood.

A blood that is strong,

Therefore I am a victor
not a victim.

Too Blessed to Be Stressed

Talk to God about it-**Blessed.**

Try to fight it alone-**Stressed.**

Staying in the word of God-**Blessed.**

Living in the flesh-**Stressed.**

Humble and content-**Blessed.**

Full of pride and greed-**Stressed.**

Knowing, this too shall pass-**Blessed.**

Living in the pains of the past-**Stressed.**

Helping others on their journey-**Blessed.**

Thinking only of self-**Stressed.**

Waiting on God-**Blessed.**

Thinking he takes too long-**Stressed.**

Talk About the Love of God

It is time to get loud about spirituality,

Whether, Muslim, Jew or Christian.

Open your mouth wherever you go

Testify of God's love to young and old.

There should be no peace or quiet,

No corner, ally, room or attic,

Void of the sound of your testimony.

Raise your voice, loud as a trumpet,

Be proud and loud,

Live for your faith, loving God out loud.

Glorify his name, as loud as you can.

It is time to get loud about our God,

Teaching is message across the land.

I want to be loud, I can no longer hold it in,

Let me tell you how good God's been.

Let me testify about my God,

Let me scream and shout,

The world should know what this love is all about.

No Walls

Jesus didn't need a fence,

He welcomed **all.**

He didn't build a wall,

His love was for us **all.**

Take the time to love **all**

The souls you meet,

Maybe you will grow to love

What makes us **all** unique.

Camouflaged

Hiding under layers of beautiful clothes,

Is a sinner so sinful, lying is all he knows.

If you see him you won't know him,

Yet he walks amongst us all,

Blending perfectly among the righteous,

Waiting to kill them all.

Though your instincts tell you,

You do not believe,

For he looks and talks and walks,

Just like you and me.

He walks among the virtuous,

Resting here and there,

Pretending to know Jesus, but he doesn't really care.

Grace

Grace is what makes you sing

Hallelujah I feel good.

Grace gives you the assurance that

Better days are coming.

Grace is dainty and unassuming,

A light that suddenly appears,

When dangers is looming.

It does not manifest in material things,

Yet, it is conspicuous in the joy it brings.

Grace means no longer accepting

The trials the world is offering.

Lone Ranger

Sometimes doing the
right thing

Will cause you to stand alone.

The walk of the righteous
is not smooth,

It is filled with curves and bumps.

Do not expect it to be easy,

Be willing to stand still,

Wait for God's instructions,

Then you can do his will.

Alone, yes, yet affixed
high above the ground.

See now, this lone ranger,

Standing on solid rock,
he knows in a battle

God has got his back.

Standing for the weak
and unprotected,

Keeping a vigilant eye.

Looking forward,
never backwards,

For yesterday is gone and done.

Today's battles are
already beginning,

The numbers are tallying up,

It seems you are winning,

For in God you placed your trust.

Shout around the
curves, and bumps

Let your voice be hear.

Being a voice for the voiceless
will sometimes mean,

Standing alone.

Humility

A prince, born in a barn,

A prince, whom many scorned.

He spent his life upon a mule

Searching for the worse among men.

Sought no riches nor power,

Sought only to honor his father.

He did not wear designer clothes,

Nor try to upgrade the mule he rode.

On a cross, where he died,

So that mankind may see the light,

An all would see and know,

Humility shall save your soul.

Value time, for it is fleeting,

Always moving, never pausing.

Value love, it is precious

It can conquer all.

The greatest man I've ever known,

Could have sat upon a throne,

Yet-he humbled himself.

Comfort Zones

It is easy it feels so good,
It's what you know and have always understood.
There are no risks here, no hurt no fear,
It makes you want to stay.

Have enough faith to leave,
For change require coming out.
You are certain to face challenges,
You might fall, fail, folly
Yet God will take you through the vail.

If you stay there, you might miss
Grace and favor to live in bliss.
Leave the comfort of what you know, and you will grow.

Guide my footsteps

Manifest it clearly, no room for doubt.

Structure a road map, showing the right path.

Guide each steps, oh lord.

Guide my steps, help me to walk in your will,

Help me to full-fill my purpose.

Guide each step oh lord.

Custody my steps oh lord,

Destiny them to my fate.

Guide each step oh lord.

Take me where you desire,

Let each step work for good.

Same

Same here, same there, same colors everywhere.

Same this, same that, same bird to watch.

So be still, why run here and there,

You will find the same things everywhere.

A new town won't make a difference,

A new school or new friends,

It's all on the earth,

And all the same in the end.

As it was said, two stanzas ago,

Be still, love where you are,

Don't run to and fro,

Happiness is not too far.

Times of Darkness

In times of darkness pray,

Ask the angels to stay,

Keep you wrapped in their wings,

Keep you from uncertain things.

In times of darkness sing,

Your voice carried on the wind,

Like a song bird sing,

Oh what joys it shall bring.

In times of darkness run,

Know that it's ok,

For those who fight and run away,

Will live to fight another day.

Tree of Temptation

Walk pass the tree
of temptation,

For it will lead you
to damnation.

Pray daily for your
salvation,

Weaponed with
determination.

Run pass the tree
of temptation,

Flee from depravation.

Showing God your
dedication

Consigning the devil
to desperation.

Fly over the tree
of temptation,

Thus, giving God
authorization.

No need for deliberation,

No preparation.

Jump over the tree
of temptation,

Less it influences
your perception.

Leaving you in need
of clarification,

Begging for emancipation.

Walk-run-fly-jump-no
passivation,

For if you are caught in
the world's depravation

Your soul faces polarization.

Be mindful of your
limitations.

Make Fear your Audience

This too shall pass Faith said,

As she tilted her head,

Looking up toward the mountain,

Knowing the journey
that laid ahead.

Fear watched as Faith walked by,

Praying to God, and all the while

Knowing God's angles
guided her steps.

Faith did not turn right nor left,

Leaving fear to see her progress.

Marching bravely to
the mountain top,

Marching quickly she
would not stop.

Fear watched in disappointment,

Hoping Faith would forfeit.

Yet Faith continued on her journey,

Fear continued to gawk and spit.

As time went on and on,

Fear became more haughty,

Thinking Faith would weaken.

Faith did not see or know,

She could not touch or confirm,

There was something
deep inside her

That beseeched her to continue
onward.

A blackish Bluish Beauty

Black is beautifully, far
from being boring.

Black has many colors,

Black, purple, blue,

All the colors you see,

When black looks back at you.

Stare now, look in wonder,

Amazed at what you see,

The most beautiful color in the world,

The color where life began.

For God spoke, saying
black is beautiful

And he so loved the world,

He gave his only son for
every black boy and girl.

Love Pass Your Hurt

It is all consuming, this thing call hurt,

Sometimes you feel like you are in the dirt.

Nothing can shake it when it comes,

But with God's grace and mercy
you will overcome.

It's possible to love, when you are hurting,

Love heals the wounds and lets God's grace in.

Love far, love near, it is all the same,

God will say love when he calls your name.

It is consuming, this thing call hurt,

The devil will use it to put you in the dirt.

He wins every time you keep hurt in,

Love pass your hurt, don't let him win

The seeds you sow, are the harvests you will reap,

Sow seeds of love and love you will receive.

Love pass your hurt, don't let the devil win,

He wants to keep you locked up in sin.

She broke you heart, a sister once close,

He broke your heart, a husband no more.

She broke your heart, a daughter who betrayed,

He broke your heart, a brother he will remain.

Love them through your pain,

God called us to love.

Love Is What It Does

Does it make you happy,

When it fills your soul?

Does it fill you with gladness,

And make you fill whole?

It's a helpful hand, or a pretty smile,

A head on a shoulder, a gentle kiss.

Love will make your breakfast,

Love will mend your clothes.

Love will hand you a tissue,

So you can blow your nose.

Love will allow you to express,

Joy, sorrow and gladness

Limitless emotions.

Love won't shut you up,

It will listen as you speak,

It only wants to help you,

It doesn't make you weak.

Love is for the hopeless,

Love is for everyone.

It doesn't matter what love says,

Just look at what it does

Father

My fathers' voice,

Oh strange to me,

It had been years

Since I last heard it.

My father's laugh

Was odd to me,

I longed for it to

Brush upon my ear.

Forgive me father

For I have sinned,

On my knees

I prayed to him.

Forgive me father,

Here I am changed,

Forgive my betrayal,

For you are the same.

It was I who left,

Your grace,

Now I hear your voice

So clearly that I raise my hand and

I cry, I cry, I CRY.

Trifecta

Mindful of my blessings.

Make every day

Into one you will

Never forget or

Deny to anyone.

Soulful joyous memories.

Scent your heart with

Odors that are

Unique in God's eyes,

Leaving good memories behind.

Body and temple are one in the same.

Before you

Over indulge

Diligently, deliberately direct

Your thoughts to something else.

Vessel

As I pull myself up from the depths of obscurity

I see the vessel with which I shall sail the ocean blue

Into fame and fortune!

A vessel procured by God,

A reward for hearing his call.

Sail on wherever I may,

Never led astray,

Calm winds, calm waves, calm water,

All orchestrated, all intentional,

His plan had been laid out,

Perfectly designed for me.

The journey continues on.

A Few Kind Words

From the mouth of babes,

The bible did say,

Comes all that is pure and true.

Oh did God one day send me an angel,

And that angel Demya was you,

Proclaimed my heart protected,

With that she stole my heart.

From the mouth of babes,

Comes only truth,

For their hearts are untainted, honest and true.

Thus now I sit and ponder,

Was it God who used her tongue,

To send me to my destiny,

His will Now I have Done.

Glad to Have You Too

This, the last, and possibly the most

Important photo in this book has

Changed everything for me. The

Caring words in this card caused an

Awakening in me the likes of which

I have never before experienced.

The author of this note also has a

Heart that is kind and pure, and

For that I hope to one day help her

Attend college. Therefore proceeds

From the sale of this book will be

Use to start a scholarship program,

#Collegesneedgoodpeopletoo# the

Program will help build good

Character in young people and

Provide financial aid for college.

The End

Printed in the United States
By Bookmasters